ZADORA
Timepieces
HAUTE HORLOGERIE

© 2007 Zadora Timepieces
Assouline Publishing
601 West 26th Street, 18th floor
New York, NY 10001, USA
Tel.: 212 989-6810 Fax: 212 647-0005
www.assouline.com

Color separation by Gravor (Switzerland)
Printed by Grafiche Milani (Italy)

ZADORA
Timepieces
HAUTE HORLOGERIE

Nicholas Foulkes

Photographs by Torkil Gudnason

ASSOULINE

andreas von Zadora-Gerlof is a name resonant with the pageantry of an age when Europe was a complex jigsaw puzzle of dukedoms and principalities, electorates and grand duchies, kingdoms and empires. The part of this polychromatic political patchwork that the Zadora-Gerlofs called home was a wild and rugged stretch of Baltic country known as Pomerania, where, in the best European fashion, they lived, hunted, collected precious objects, and continued their military traditions. For centuries life followed the same pattern, and had World War II not intervened, Andreas von Zadora-Gerlof would probably be sitting on his ancestral lands, planning his next shooting party or pondering what trinkets or bibelots he should add to his family's collection of art and objets d'art.

History however took a different turn: Pomerania became part of Poland and found itself on the wrong side of the Iron Curtain. Instead of being groomed to take over running the family's estates in the Baltic lands, young Andreas found himself growing up on the other side of the world, literally, on Queen Charlotte Island, in an archipelago near Vancouver, British Columbia, and Alaska, with just family stories, old portraits and one or two pieces of Fabergé to remind him of a life he only knew from what his father told him.

1

ife on these remote Canadian islands was lived outdoors and the young von Zadora-Gerlof spent his time hunting with the indigenous peoples. Hunting was a passion but not without its dangers, as he discovered at age 12. "I was gutting a deer and the knife slipped while I was trying to get through the sternum. My hand slipped over the blade and the three small fingers were cut to the bone. I washed it in the creek, and later the hospital sewed it up. I had almost severed the fingers, and they were never able to bend after that. Then, about two years later, I was hunting with my Indian friend, and I was sneaking up on a deer that was going to the beach to lick the salt. I was crawling along trying to get a shot, and in British Columbia we have huge waves and tides, which throw up big logs and driftwood onto the beach. My friend, who was also sneaking up on the deer, knocked a log down onto me. I was knocked out, and it crushed my arm, which swelled up."

Medical care on this remote island in the late 1960s and early 1970s was basic. The doctor misdiagnosed a broken arm and put the limb in a cast, and rather than heal itself, the arm continued to swell, leaving the young Zadora-Gerlof in agony. "One of the nurses noticed that my hand was going black and cut away some of the plaster, which saved my arm from being finished that night." He managed to hang on to his arm—just barely. "By the time they noticed their mistake, my hand had literally withered to a bird claw, and I couldn't move anything. The tendons were now fore-shortened." Conventional physical therapy was tedious and had little effect. It was then that the father of his hunting companion suggested something different.

"He said, 'Why doesn't he hold an adze and do some totem pole carving and metal engraving?' I took to it like a fish to water, particularly the gold and silver engraving, and quickly became good at it. I soon started sculpting in wood, then bronze, and then I began sculpting gems."

today Andreas von Zadora-Gerlof is a world-renowned maker of objects of virtu and has been described as America's Fabergé. Sculpting stones of near diamond hardness, he releases forms from these minerals as diverse as frogs and falcons, pegasi and pigs. Technically brilliant and artistically inspired, he has proved himself a master of the glyptic arts and a truly gifted individual. When he looks at a stone, whether it is a piece of jade or a huge block of rock crystal, he sees not simply a stone, but what is within, be it a life-size swan, an iguana, or a tiny scarab, waiting to be liberated. In his role as a designer, von Zadora-Gerlof has assembled a school of craftsmen to take care of every detail, however humble. His apprentices and collaborators work in disciplines as diverse as enameling, repoussé, engraving, goldsmithing, and micro-engineering to help him realize objects as complex as full-size automated animals crafted from precious metals that mimic life itself.

almost forty years after he discovered his talent for carving stone, his passion has not dimmed if anything, it has intensified. His elegant nineteenth-century apartment in London's Mayfair district is an eloquent testimony to his continuing love affair with exotic minerals. The ambience is part stately home (the walls are crowded with heraldic escutcheons and ancestral portraits) and part geological museum. Against the fireplace leans a striated slab of fossilized wood, its tiger-striped honey-colored variegation catching the shafts of sunlight that pierce the still air. A large table is strewn with minerals: watermelon tourmaline that is both green and pink; warm whiskey-toned chunks of citrine that seem to glow with an inner light; green beryl with the lucid brightness of boiled sweets; opalescent-flecked labradorite; Caribbean-clear aquamarine; the haunting blue of lapis lazuli which moved Yeats to poetry; the enigmatic green of jade; and a hunk of quartz with a wisp of cool clear gray at its center, as if a plume of celestial cigar smoke has been trapped within.

It is from these exotic and enticing stones that Zadora coaxes the objects to be found in homes everywhere, from the ranches of cattle barons to the castles of princes, delighting international patrons as diverse as movie stars and business moguls. When one examines his work with precious and semiprecious stones, his exquisite fashioning of coveted metals and his enameling, one can easily see why he has been compared to Carl Fabergé. Anyone who has seen the palaces of the czars, the churches of St. Petersburg, and the treasures of the Hermitage will recognize the variety of color, texture, and feeling in Zadora's work.

To the uninitiated he opens up the world of hard stones. Such is his dexterity and genius for bringing out the subtleties and the seemingly infinite varieties of these exotic-sounding stones, that mere diamonds seem somehow quotidian. Zadora is certainly one the world's leading gemstone sculptors. However, to view him solely as such is to miss the subtlety and diversity of what he has achieved.

t he key is to understand that the man is at least as multi-faceted as the pieces he creates. Knowing the delicacy of Zadora's work, and the sensitivity of his animal sculptures, one might be surprised to learn that he remains keen on hunting and, although he turned his back on his family's military tradition, he did indeed graduate from one of America's most prestigious military academies. He is also exceedingly proud, in his quiet understated way, of his black belt in karate. This determined side of his character saw him through the early years of his life as a glyptic artist, which was very much in defiance of the family's traditional military aspirations.

Happily, Zadora's talent was appreciated by influential patrons. When he was not yet out of his twenties, his reputation was such that when Ward Landrigan of Verdura was looking for someone to make items of jewelry that the great Fulco di Verdura had sketched, but that had never been made, he turned to Zadora. Sold-out exhibitions in New York and Paris of Zadora's own work followed and in Paris, on the morning after one of his shows, he met the woman who would become his wife.

"I had a hangover like you wouldn't believe," he remembers. "So I stumbled out the door and headed toward the Eiffel Tower. I walked and walked, and finally ended up sitting in a restaurant in the Trocadero. As I was walking, I saw the most beautiful girl I'd ever seen in my life. I thought, 'If you don't go back and introduce yourself you're going to hate yourself forever.'"

Luckily, Andreas von Zadora did indeed go back, and introduced himself to that beautiful girl, Monica, who is now his wife. Today Monica holds a vital position within the company. An accomplished artist in her own right, she translates her husband's ideas into beautiful drawings, enabling the clients and the craftsmen to envision exactly what work of art is planned.

by the time Zadora reached his thirties, he seemed to be at the top of his career: he was a critical and commercial success who had not only gained the respect of his professional peers, but also enjoyed a full order book and a busy workshop employing a number of skilled craftsmen to assist him. This chain of command allowed Zadora to concentrate on the demanding detailed work, the deft touches that brought his pieces to life, and also gave him time to nurture more ambitious projects. He was keen to push the limits of his expertise beyond the netsuke-like animals, small sculptures, Fabergé-inspired objets d'art, and portrait cameos for which he had become famous.

During this period, the epithet "America's Fabergé", became well-known as Zadora took commissions from the leading industrial, agricultural, and financial dynasties of America. The late 1980s was a heady and frenetic period. Like in England during the nineteenth century, or Russia during the time the czars, fortunes were made or dramatically enlarged, and a statement piece from Zadora became de rigueur for many.

Often when talking of the pieces that he creates for clients, Zadora speaks of collaborating with his patrons. As the commissions he worked on became increasingly ambitious in scale and creative scope, so they also became more personal to the clients who bespoke them. It could be as straightforward as a sculpture of a particularly cherished animal, or it could have a deeper psychological significance. as was the case with Zadora's first automated object, made for an individual he describes as "a publishing titan in Minnesota."

As a child, this man had endured poverty. Among the hurts that remained with him into adult life was that during his childhood he had never been able to afford to ride on a carousel. Perhaps in part because he so wanted to pay for those merry-go-round rides, the penniless child had grown into a rich and powerful man, a rich and powerful man still haunted by a joyless childhood. He turned to Zadora to help him lay that particular ghost to rest.

The result was a superb carousel created from a veritable lapidary lexicon that included aquamarine-morganite, beryl, citrine, diamonds, gold, lapis lazuli, malachite, orthoclase, pink quartz, rock crystal, rhodochrosite, rubellite, rubies, rutilated quartz, sapphires, and smoky quartz. The detail, right down to the tiny lightbulbs strung around the carousel canopy, is impeccable. But the carefully carved individual creatures—part mythical part heraldic, part comic book, and in every way true to the full-size fairground originals—are what bring the piece to life…and the complex mechanics, which rotate the piece while moving the individual sculptures up and down and activating the accompanying music. Just as Citizen Kane had his Rosebud, so this man had his Zadora carousel.

Zadora of course had been known in New York, but a show at the Forbes Magazine Galleries propelled both his reputation and his business to a new level. Malcom Forbes had been introduced to Zadora via Eleanor Lambert, and the reference to Lambert is significant in that for years she decreed who was in, and who was out of style, with the publication of her annual best-dressed list. As America's arbiter elegantiarum of that time, this grande dame's endorsement was crucial when it came to the world of fashion and society.

This was another defining period for Zadora, and among the commissions that followed was his most ambitious and expensive: a series of clocks inspired by the George Delacorte Musical Clock in New York's Central Park. Created for the Johnson family (eponymous founders of the Johnson & Johnson), once again this was the sort of commission that had a deep emotional significance for the patron, the family's matriarch, who wanted one of the five-feet-high timepieces for herself and another three for her children. Complete with a hardstone clock tower, dancing animals playing delicately enameled musical instruments, monkeys hammering a bell, and sprays of followers, the petals painstakingly carved from vibrant, semiprecious stones, each was made unique through the use of different combinations of stones, and the result was a quartet of elaborate and whimsical items that entered the realms of the fantastic on the hour every hour, playing Beethoven's *Ode to Joy* to mark the passing of another 60 minutes.

Since then, the imaginative scope and the sheer scale of the pieces envisioned by Zadora has increased dramatically. Where his pieces were once solely escapist fantasies, it is possible to see a more mystical side to his work. For instance, he is not afraid to confront mortality and has created a series of full-size human skulls hewn from block minerals.

As fate would decree, however, a collaboration with the entrepreneur and venture-capitalist H. Joachim von der Goltz gave birth to the most innovative and spectacular timepiece to burst upon the horological scene to date: the Zadora Timepiece.

For some time, in addition to exploring the cutting edge of robotics and creating objects that give the appearance of life, Zadora had immersed himself in the historically rich culture of horology, creating timepieces that have become progressively more involved and complex. His clocks range from the playful exuberance of the 1997 Rhinoceros Clock, sculpted from opalescent labradorite, upon which two monkeys perch, to the truly remarkable Four Seasons Clock. More than a timepiece, the Four Seasons Clock is a complex piece of micromechanical engineering that encompasses an assembly of revolving enameled eggs, each of which opens to reveal an automated scene such as flowers growing or chicks hatching. It is the sort of object that would, no doubt, have delighted the Romanovs and would been proudly displayed in the Winter Palace or in their summer residence at Tsarkoe Seloe.

however, one form of timepiece above all others seemed to captivate Zadora: the orbital clock. In this design, a rotating cylindrical dial revolves on a horizontal axis allowing the time to be read at a fixed point. H. Joachim von der Goltz suggested that Zadora create a wristwatch using the cylindrical dial, enabling the wearer to read the time from the side. This would then release the hitherto function of the face from time-telling to provide a platform upon which to display an exquisite piece of Zadora's sculpted art.

The move into wristwatches seemed natural, and the success of Zadora's standing clocks indicated that focusing attention on the wrist would echo that would have clients clamouring for different ways to display his art.

The cylindrical mechanism is one to which Zadora has returned time and time again. The unique configuration of this particular timepiece allows for all manner of decorative enhancement, as it provides a flat surface on top of the revolving cylinder, which Zadora lost no time in exploiting to the fullest extent. Whether finished in guilloche enamel and topped with one of Zadora's hallmark animal sculptures, or simply used as the base for more ambitious tableaux, such as the citrine bear reaching up a golden bough to steal some honey from a bees nest (the individual bees being capable of use as brooches).

The first challenge to be faced was how to miniaturize the orbital clock and adapt it for the wrist, an idea that subsequently received a patent. Inspired by the study of some of the earliest sixteenth-century personal timepieces, which were drumlike and worn around the neck, these were items of jewelry that also happened to tell time, and this concept especially appealed to Zadora's philosophy of luxury.

t his daring innovation allowed an unlimited scope for the personalization of the watch, whether mounted by one of Zadora's playful animals or whimsical abstractions, ensuring that each and every watch is unique unto its wearer and collector.

While the drumlike design of the Zadora watch will appeal to those connoisseurs familiar with the history of horology; it is the innovative readout of the time through the side of the case that accounts for its arresting visual appeal.

Just as he releases the creatures that he sees within blocks of hardstone, so the challenge that Andreas von Zadora set himself was to free the jewelry watch from the constraints of centuries of dogma that have dictated that the flat, uppermost surface of the watch, be devoted to giving a readout of the time. Whether the time is given by hands moving around a dial, or the jump hour method whereby the number of the hours and minutes appear in small windows; the potential for personal expression offered by a wristwatch has been restricted to mere dial decoration. By creating a cylindrical platformed timepiece, where the drumlike "dial" rotates and the "hand" remains fixed, and where the central portion of the case is transparent; Zadora has given himself the opportunity to develop the top of the watch as a thing of beauty.

however, Zadora has had to accustom himself to working on an extremely small scale, and within the constraints of the watch remaining wearable. "I have had to miniaturize the presentation that I give on a clock, " he says. "With so much of my work, I can have as much room as I want. A watch is so much smaller. You have to microsize everything." This challenge has meant that Zadora will often devote an entire day to modeling the motif that is to appear on the head of a single watch to make sure that the design fits on the tiny platform. He is equally painstaking when it comes to selecting the stone that will enable him to realize his artistic intention.

"I need stones that read beautifully on a much smaller scale. For example, the turtle needed a hot orange color; a more subtle citrine would not work. With the watches, I find myself working with more gemlike material that is almost facet grade."

Even the most quotidian elements of the Zadora Timepiece have been worked on to maximize their aesthetic potential: the winding and setting crown carries a briolette-cut diamond, the lugs are expertly set with precious stones, and located between them is the time indicator. This triangular diamond marks the passage of time on the rotating hand-engraved dial, which is itself set with small diamonds marking the half hours.

The hand-wound movement, with a *reserve de marche* of 36 hours, which powers this unique horological jeu d'esprit has been specially developed in the best Swiss 'manufacture' tradition by a small team of artisans in the Swiss Jura. In its purest form, this "manufacture" ethos dictates that all the watch components, from springs to wheels to bridges, are designed, manufactured, chamfered, polished, decorated, assembled, and mounted in-house, featuring a Zadora Timepiece 01 Calibre movement.

S uch a demanding and time-consuming process requires highly skilled watchmakers working in a rarefied atmosphere and is diametrically opposed to the principles of mass production. Blackened steel components are hand-polished for hours until they reach perfection, in just the same way that a jeweler would work with materials many hundreds of times more valuable. Even those components that will only ever be seen by a watchmaker repairing or servicing the watch are decorated with the tiny circular engraving known as perlage, while the bridges that keep the movement in place carry the delicate stripes of the Côtes de Genève style of engraving. A small team working according to the high standards of the manufacture system is able to create only a handful of movements in the course of a year. "I had to learn that just the manufacture of the watch took an awful long time; that gear-up time does not exist for me with sculptures. I was impressed by the skill of procurement—the parts are difficult to make, and even the galuchat of the straps has to be specially selected and cut. There are so many disciplines involved that even though a wristwatch is a small object, it takes that much longer to realize the finished article."

t o examine for a minute the vulgar consideration of cost, the manufacture process is an expensive one, even when creating a conventional mechanical movement. When added to the cost of researching, designing, and developing—inventing in fact—a new movement capable of powering this innovative concept, the result is a precious example of mechanical ingenuity that only a few fortunate individuals will ever be able to enjoy.

In establishing the movement of the Zadora watch, the watchmaker has challenged more than just the aesthetics of timekeeping. The movement has been designed so that when the time comes for servicing (after three years or so, the lubricants in the movement become more viscous, and accuracy can be affected), it can be dismantled from the top, enabling the watchmaker to remove the winding step through the upper part of the watch.

The beauty of the Zadora watch is therefore as much internal as exterior. The difference is that while others may be able to appreciate the manifestation of Zadora's mastery of the glyptic arts, only the owner of this unique object will truly learn to understand and appreciate the genius of Zadora the watchmaker. This daring concept allows a hitherto unimaginable scope for the personalization of the appearance of the watch, whether through one of Zadora's playful animals or the macabre memento-mori-style ornamentation of a skull. Indeed, the creation of a Zadora Timepiece is a collaboration between artist and patron, and Zadora may suggest anything from a scorpion to a slice of water-melon as an appropriate decorative motif.

"This work is very custom-order driven, so I rely on being inspired by the clients," Zadora explains. "A watch really is a personal item, and a Zadora watch appeals to people who want something bespoke, a custom piece that they can't find anywhere else. It is for somebody who wants to add something different to a personal collection, something not seen in every corner of the world. It is truly that person's watch, and there will be no other exactly like it. It is unique to its owner."

Only thirty Zadora Timepieces will be produced per annum. To behold this marvel of invention with its cylindrical dial and exquisitely embellished top, one can truly say the Zadora Time-piece has changed the Face of Time!

Fig. 2.

Fig. 1.

Fig. 8.

Fig. 9.

Fig. 7.

Fig. 6.

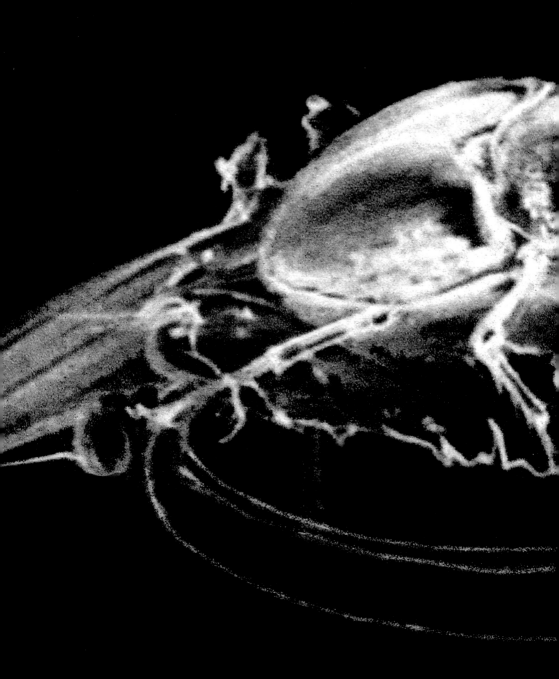

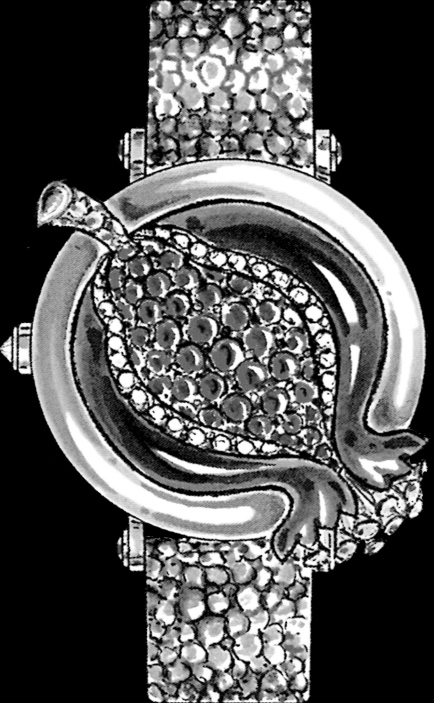

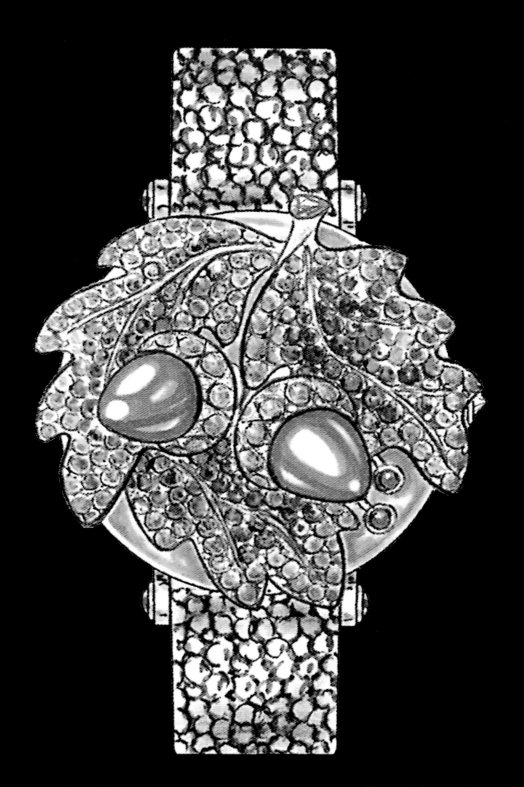

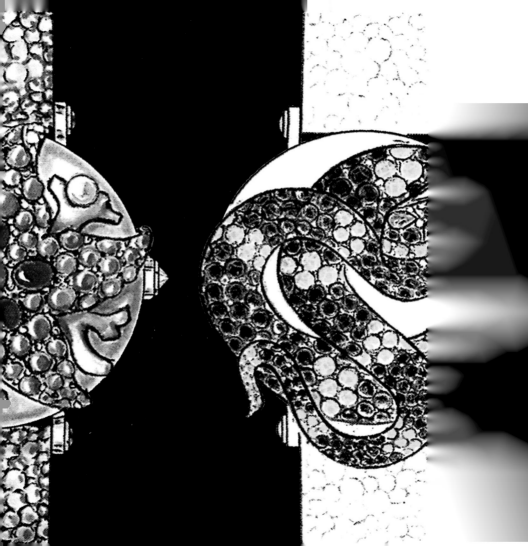

Where Zadora's pieces were once solely escapist fantasies it is possible to see a more mystical side to his work.

Zadora has immersed
himself in the historically rich
culture of horology;
creating timepieces that have
become progressively
more involved and complex.

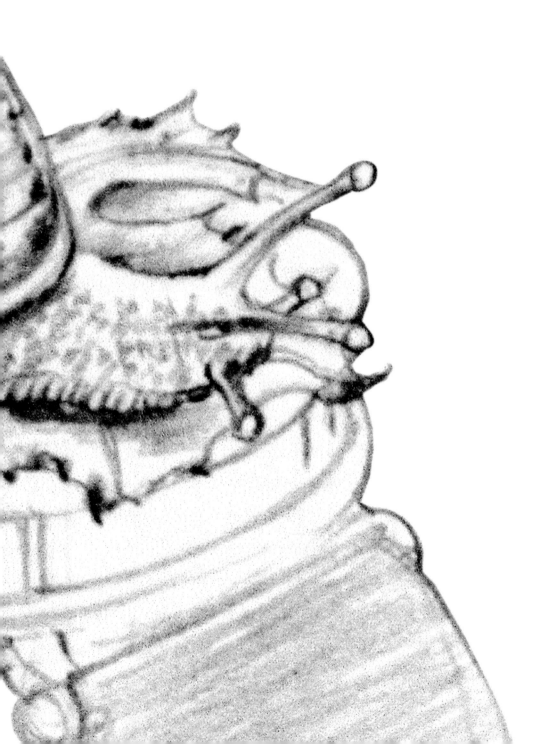

Just as he releases the
creatures that he sees within
blocks of hardstone, so
Zadora has been able to free
the jewelry watch
from the constraints of
centuries of dogma that have
dictated that the flat, uppermost surface of the
watch be devoted to giving
a readout of the time.

As one would expect from
a Zadora piece, even
the most quotidian elements of
the watch have been
worked to maximize their
aesthetic potential.

Zadora Timepieces

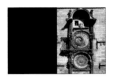

The Astronomical Clock on the Old Town Hall, Prague. 16th century. © Erich Lessing/Art Resource, New York.

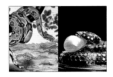

Reptiles and insects from Albert Seba's *Locupletissimi Rerum Naturalim,* ca.1750. © British Museum, London, Great Britain/Art Resource. **Zadora Snake Timepiece:** Pavé black and canary yellow diamonds dress the magnificent creature. In patinated palladium 18kt white gold, the serpent proudly bares pear-shaped emerald eyes and clutches a baroque South Sea pearl in its mouth. 18kt white gold case. Price: $150,000 USD

Zadora Snake Timepiece: Pavé black and canary yellow diamonds dress the magnificent creature. In patinated palladium 18kt white gold, the serpent proudly bares pear shaped emerald eyes and clutches a baroque South Sea pearl in its mouth. 18kt white gold case. Price: $150,000 USD

The Dream by Henri Rousseau. 1910. Oil on canvas. © The Museum of Modern Art/Licensed by SCALA/Art Resource, NY.

Zadora Frog Prince Timepiece: This 18kt yellow gold royal amphibian showcases diamond studded feet and ruby cabochon eyes and proudly wears a diamond-encrusted crown. Tsavorites cover the pavé Prince studded with blue sapphire cabochons. 18kt yellow gold case. Price: $150,000 USD

Zadora Frog Prince Timepiece: Price: $150,000 USD

Beatle Inverted: Illustration © Monica von Zadora-Gerlof.

Pomegranate. Acorn: Illustration © Monica von Zadora-Gerlof.

Zadora Acorns & Oak Leaves Timepiece: In patinated 18kt white gold, multi-colored sapphires adorn the pavé leaves, in green tourmalines and brown and white diamonds. Brown diamonds accent the acorn nuts of sculpted amber-colored citrine. 18kt yellow gold case. Price: $150,000 USD

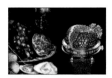

Still Life with Fruit and Acorns by Rachel Ruysch, ca. 1716; © Christie's Images/Corbis. Zadora Pomegranate Timepiece: This fruit of the gods, in 18kt yellow gold, is pavé set with green tsavorites, ruby cabochons, and white diamond details; brown and yellow diamonds decorate the stem. The fruit also doubles as a delightful pillbox via a concealed center opening. 18kt yellow gold case. Price: $150,000 USD

Scorpian, star, and snake: Illustration © Monica von Zadora-Gerlof.

Zadora Scorpion Timepiece: The scorpion crouches on a guilloche top claiming ruby eyes and a rubellite stinger. In 18kt white gold, he is also set in micro pavé grey and white diamonds. 18kt white gold case. Price: $150,000 USD

Saint Jerome Writing by Caravaggio, 1606. Photographed by Mauro Magliani, 1997 © Alinari/Corbis

Zadora Skull Timepiece: In hand hammered and textured 18kt white gold, the gleaming skull is partly buried amid a multi-gem encrusted surface of textured yellow gold, emeralds, rubies, sapphires, amethysts, and diamonds of various shapes and sizes. 18kt white gold case. Price: $150,000 USD

Sunflower: Illustration © Monica von Zadora-Gerlof.

Exotic Landscape by **Henri Rousseau.** 1910. Oil on canvas. © Norton Simon Collection, The Bridgeman Art Library

Zadora Poppy Flower Timepiece: In platinum and palladium 18kt white gold, the flower is set in pavé pink and white diamonds, rubies, and pink sapphires. These intricate details offer an ombré effect to its voluptuous petals and pistils, in black patina on platinum. 18kt white gold case. Price: $150,000 USD

Zadora Enamel Guilloche Timepiece: This elegant watch, in 18kt yellow gold and a royal blue enameled guilloche disk, is set in white diamonds and surrounds a large green cabochon tsavorite center stone. 18kt yellow gold case. Price: $95,000.00 USD

An illustration of sea life from an edition of Meyers Konversations-Lexikon, a nineteenth-century German encyclopedia;1895. © Swim Ink/Corbis.

Zadora Starfish Timepiece: The tropical treasure, in 18kt white gold, is pavé set in degradé blue sapphires and sprinkled with large blue cabochon sapphires. Coral branches frame the pavéd white diamond underside.18kt white gold case. Price: $150,000 USD

Snail: Illustration © Monica von Zadora-Gerlof.

Zadora Ladybug Timepiece: This harbinger of good luck, in textured 18kt yellow gold, is micro-pavé set with richly colored rubies and black diamonds. Cabochon emeralds for eyes add distinguished detail. 18kt yellow gold case.
Price: $150,000 USD

Zadora Ladybug Timepiece: Price: $150,000 USD

Zadora Queen Bee Timepiece: The 18kt yellow gold empress, with ruby cabochon eyes, wears a multi-gem encrusted crown and hovers over yellow and white diamond pavé honey cells. Canary yellow diamonds decorate her body while white diamonds encrust her wings. 18kt yellow gold case. Price: $150,000 USD

Tortoises Swimming among Marine Plants by Totoya Hokkei ca.1800-1850 © Brooklyn Museum/Corbis

Zadora Sea Turtle Timepiece: Light brown pavé diamonds cover this ancient symbol of wisdom, in textured 18kt yellow gold. Its citrine shell is minutely sculpted, and its eyes are made of cabochon emeralds. 18kt yellow gold case.
Price: $150,000 USD